Jethro & Co.

Jethro & Co.

Carine Mackenzie

CHRISTIAN FOCUS PUBLICATIONS

ISBN 1 85792 057 0

Published by
Christian Focus Publications
Geanies House, Fearn, Tain, Ross-shire
IV20 1TW, Scotland, Great Britain

Cover design by Donna Macleod
Cover illustration by Mike Gordon

Printed and bound in Great Britain by
Cox & Wyman Ltd, Reading, Berks

Contents

INTRODUCTION

Every story in the Bible has been given to us for a purpose. Some characters are very well known, like Moses and David and Paul. But others are not so well known. We are going to look at some of these less well known characters and see what we can learn from them.

Insert the missing vowels in the text

a a a a a a

e e e e e e e e

i i i i i i i i i i

o o o o

u u u u

_ ll Scr _ ptur _ _s G _ d

br _ _ thed

_ nd _s _ s _ f _ l f _ r t _ _ ch _ ng,

r _ b _ k _ ng,

c _ rr _ ct _ ng, _ nd tr _ _ n _ ng _ n

r _ ght _ _ _ sn _ ss.

AMRAM AND JOCHABED

Exodus 1-2

Amram and his wife, Jochabed, were Israelites who lived in Egypt. The king made all the Israelite people his slaves. They had to work very hard making bricks and working in the fields. Their masters were very cruel.

The king was afraid that the Israelite people would take over his land. He gave the wicked order - 'Every baby boy born to the Israelite women must be thrown into the River Nile.'

Amram and Jochabed had a little baby boy. They hid him in the house for three months. Then it was difficult to keep the secret. Jochabed made a little basket, and laid her baby boy in it. The basket was carefully placed among the reeds on the water of the River Nile. Big sister was put on guard.

The princess went down to the river to bathe. She noticed the basket and sent a servant to fetch it. When it was opened, the baby began to cry and the princess felt very sorry for him.

Big sister offered to go and fetch a nurse for the baby and the princess agreed at once. The baby was adopted by the princess and looked after by the nurse. Who was she? Jochabed - his mother.

What was the name of the baby?

Colour in the areas *__without__* *a dot to find the name.*

JETHRO

Exodus 18

Jethro was a wise man living in Midian. His daughter was married to Moses. When Moses was camping in the desert, Jethro came to visit him. Moses told Jethro everything that God had done for him and his people - how he had saved them from the Egyptians and led them all the way.

Jethro gave Moses good advice about his work. 'Get capable men to help you,' he suggested. 'Don't do all the work yourself, but make the difficult decisions.'

Moses took Jethro's advice, and his work load became lighter.

What did Jethro say? Starting at P, work round the tent, taking every third letter until all are used up.

P_____ __ __ ___ ____

___ _ ____ ____ ___ ____

__ _____ ___ ____ ___ ___

_____ ____. (Exodus 18:10-11)

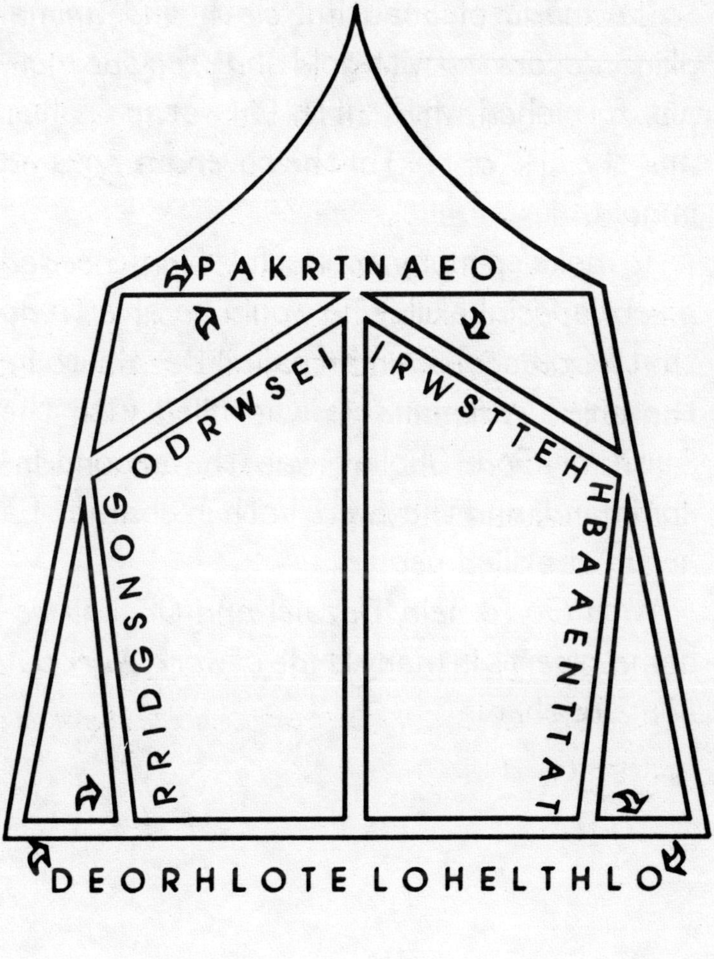

BEZALEL AND OHOLIAB

Exodus 35-38

God instructed Moses to make a tabernacle or special tent as a place of worship. It was to be made of beautiful cloth and animal skins, decorated with gold and precious metals, furnished with table, lampstand, altar and the ark (or box) of the covenant covered in gold.

To make so many wonderful things needed a very special skill. Who would be able to do that? God chose a man called Bezalel to be the chief workman. He was filled with the Spirit of God. Oholiab was the second-in-command, and they were both in charge of a group of skilled people.

With God's help, Bezalel and Oholiab became experts in many kinds of work. Work out some of them.

Match up the shapes to make the word.

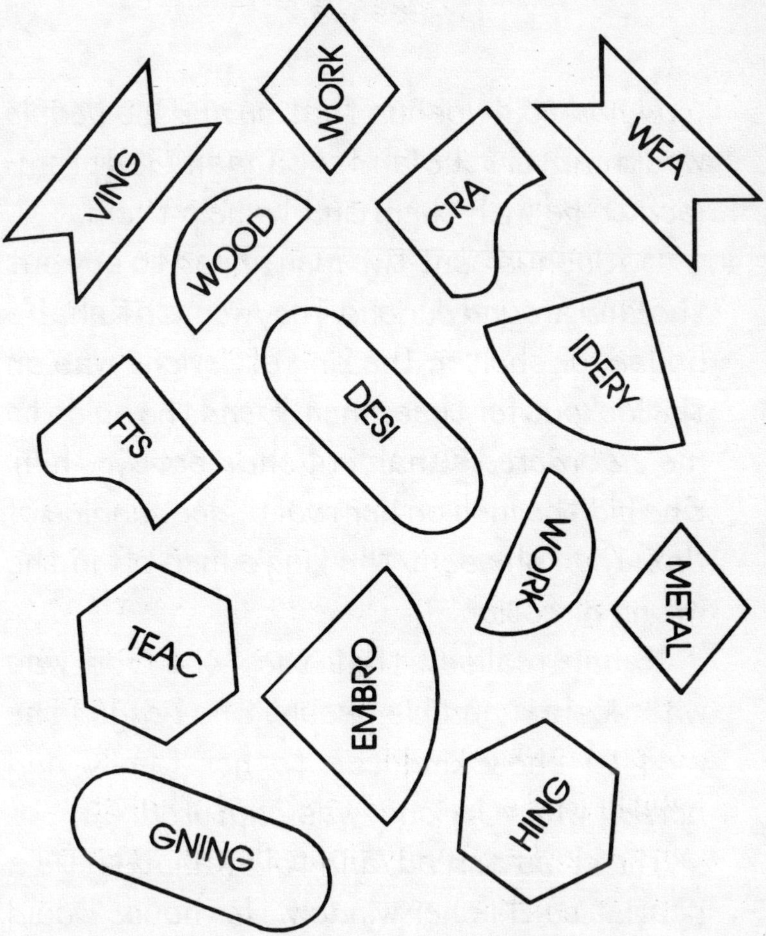

When everything was finished, Moses inspected the work. They had done it all just as the Lord had commanded. So Moses blessed them.

RAHAB

Joshua 2

God had told Joshua that he and his people would capture the land of Canaan. God promised to be with them and to help them.

So Joshua sent two men ahead to spy out the land around Jericho. They went to Rahab's house for shelter. The king of Jericho was on the lookout for these men. 'Send the spies to me,' he ordered Rahab, but she disobeyed him. She hid the men on her roof under bundles of flax. Then she sent the king's men off in the wrong direction.

Rahab realised that the Lord God was with Joshua and his people. She begged the men to show kindness to her family and herself when Jericho was captured.

The spies agreed, and told Rahab to tie a scarlet cord in her window. Her house would then be safe.

The men escaped from the roof by rope and returned to Joshua and the other Israelites.

Rahab confessed her faith in God. Begin at T and work your way round in a clockwise direction to find out what she said?

D	Y	O	U	R	G	O
R	B	O	V	E	A	D
O	A	B	E	L	N	I
L	N	H		O	D	S
E	E	T		W	O	G
H	V	R	A	E	N	O
T	A	E	H	N	I	D

↑

___ ____ ____ ___ __ ___ __

______ _____ ___ __ _____ _____

ACHAN

Joshua 7

God helped the people of Israel to conquer the city of Jericho. All the gold and silver and precious things that were captured belonged to God only - they were to be put into the treasury. One man called Achan disobeyed the order. Because of his sin the whole nation suffered.

On the next campaign to capture the town of Ai, the Israelite army was completely defeated and chased back. The people could hardly believe what had happened. Why hadn't God helped them?

Joshua, the leader, prayed and asked God for an explanation.

'Someone has stolen from me and lied about it,' said God. 'That is why your army was defeated. Find out who is guilty and deal with him.'

Early next morning Joshua gathered the people together. The culprit was narrowed down to one tribe, then one clan, then one family until Achan was discovered to be guilty. He confessed to having stolen a beautiful robe, some silver and gold, and hiding them underground in his tent. The goods were recovered and Achan was punished by being stoned to death.

After the sin was dealt with, God encouraged Joshua to march against Ai again. This time they were successful.

God's message is written backwards here. Decode it and write it properly below.

oD ton eb

degaruocsid eb ton od :diarfa

-- --- -- ------- --

--- -- -----------

Our sin affects our lives too. The only thing we can do is to ask the Lord Jesus to forgive our sins and to wash away all our guilt.

MEPHIBOSHETH

2 Samuel 9

David was a great friend of Jonathan, King Saul's son. Even when Saul was trying to kill David, Jonathan helped him to escape.

After Jonathan and Saul had been killed, David became king. King David prospered and defeated many of his enemies, but he did not forget his friend, Jonathan. 'Is there any member of Saul's family left?' he asked one day. 'I would like to show him kindness for my friend Jonathan's sake.'

Enquiries were made. News was brought to King David.

'Jonathan's son is still alive. He is lame in both feet. His name is Mephibosheth.'

His story was very tragic. When the boy's nurse heard of the death of Saul and Jonathan in battle, she picked him up and ran to hide. In her hurry, she dropped 5 year old Mephibosheth and he was crippled.

Mephibosheth was brought to King David.

What did David say to him? Pick out every third letter and find out.

R	W	D	G	E	O	L	B	N	X	R	O	Q	D
T	Q	Y	B	D	X	E	M	R	A	V	B	F	S
G	R	F	F	A	K	Y	I	M	P	D	T	W	F
H	J	O	T	L	R	A	Z	I	N	Z	W	I	J
I	P	H	L	M	L	L	B	W	S	V	J	U	H
G	R	C	X	E	N	C	L	S	K	Y	R	Q	S
Y	V	H	S	V	O	C	E	W	N	C	Y	P	G
O	K	Z	U	K	J	K	F	D	I	M	N	N	R
H	D	F	A	N	B	D	E	E	L	S	P	T	S

__ ___ __ _______ ___ _

____ _______ ____ ___

____

What special privilege did Mephibosheth have? Work out the code.

A	B	C	D	E	F	G	H	I	J	K	L	M
1	2	3	4	5	6	7	8	9	10	11	12	13

N	O	P	Q	R	S	T	U	V	W	X	Y	Z
14	15	16	17	18	19	20	21	22	23	24	25	26

8. 5.   1. 12. 23. 1. 25. 19.   1. 20. 5.   1. 20.

_ _   _ _ _ _ _ _   _ _ _   _ _

20. 8. 5.   1. 9. 14. 7. 19.   20. 1. 2. 12. 5.

_ _ _   _ _ _ _ _   _ _ _ _ _

NATHAN

2 Samuel 12

Nathan was a wise prophet and a friend of King David. David had sinned very seriously by taking someone else's wife as his own. God told Nathan to go and confront the king with this sin. Nathan went to David and told him a story, about a man who had lots of sheep and cattle. When the man's friend came to visit, he took a poor neighbour's only pet lamb to make a meal for the visitor. David was very indignant at this behaviour. 'He should be made to pay back four times over,' he declared, 'and then put to death.'

Nathan spoke boldly to the king, 'You are the man,' he said.

God had given so much to David yet he had taken another man's wife to be his own.

Nathan's plain speaking made David realise that he had been sinful. He confessed to God and was forgiven. David wrote Psalm 51 as a humble prayer for forgiveness.

Slot the pieces into place and find out what David said in verse 2 of the psalm.

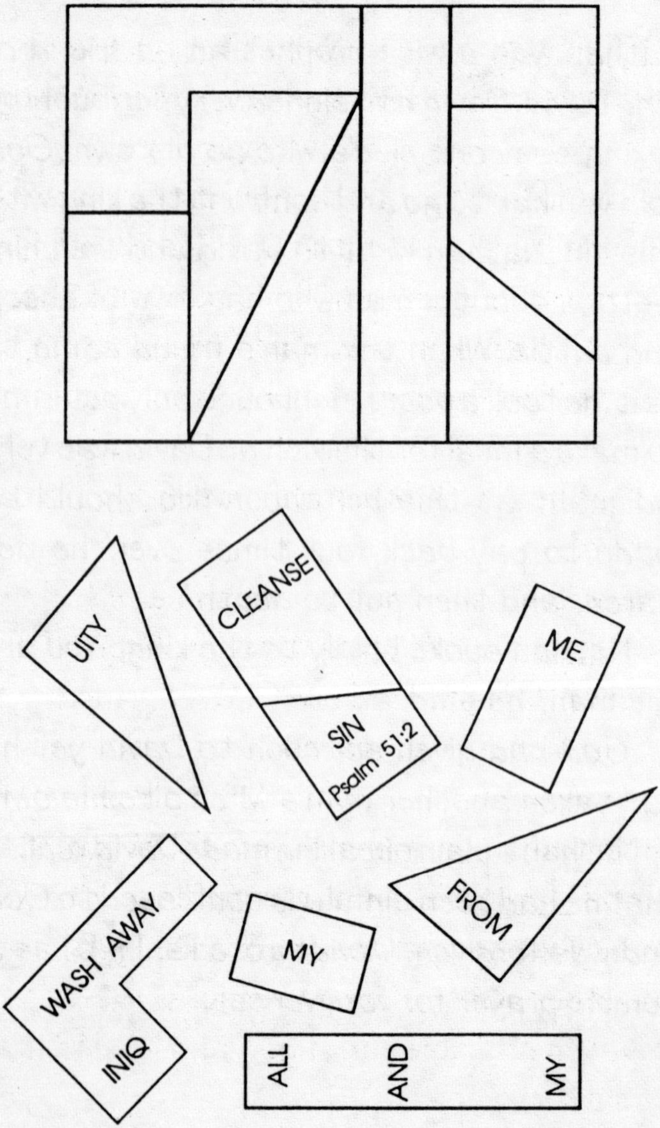

ABIGAIL

1 Samuel 25

Abigail was a beautiful and intelligent woman, who was married to a bad-tempered, mean man called Nabal. He was very wealthy, and owned lots of goats and sheep.

King David was out in the desert with his warriors. He sent ten of his men with greetings to Nabal, who was nearby shearing his sheep. 'Remind him that we were favourable towards his flocks and servants said David. Ask if he can give us whatever food he can spare.'

David's men were not well received; Nabal was rude and insulting to them. When he was told what Nabal had said, David armed 400 of his men and prepared to attack.

In the meantime, one of Nabal's servants reported the whole incident to Abigail. She was a clever woman and immediately worked out what might happen. She gathered together plenty of food - bread, wine, mutton, roasted grain, raisins, figs - and loaded it all on to donkeys.

Abigail rode with the supplies and when she met King David and his men, she dismounted and bowed down to the king. She begged him not to kill any of her family and to ignore Nabal's foolish action. Her words were so wise that David was completely won over. Her quick-witted action had saved her family and had prevented unnecessary bloodshed.

Later, Abigail's husband Nabal died suddenly, and David asked Abigail to be his wife.

The words underlined in the story are hidden in the grid on page 23. Can you find them? The remaining letters tell us one of the nice things that Abigail said to David.

____

____

____

1 Samuel 25:29

I	Y	O	L	I	A	G	I	B	A	U
R	N	L	I	F	E	W	D	I	L	L
B	R	T	N	A	B	A	L	O	E	B
O	U	E	E	N	D	S	E	C	O	U
E	R	D	V	L	E	L	Y	I	N	F
D	T	A	H	E	L	B	R	E	A	D
U	E	V	B	U	L	I	N	D	L	E
R	O	I	F	T	H	C	G	E	L	I
V	I	D	N	G	B	Y	T	E	H	E
G	R	E	E	T	I	N	G	S	N	L
O	R	D	Y	O	U	R	G	O	D	T

JABEZ

1 Chronicles 4:9-10

The first few chapters of 1 Chronicles give the names of those who were descended from great men like Noah, Abraham, Israel and David. In the middle of the list we read about a man called JABEZ. He was more honourable than his brothers. His mother called him Jabez (which sounds like the Hebrew word for 'pain') because she gave birth to him in pain.

Jabez cried out to God in prayer. The Bible tells us what this prayer was.

Change the symbols for the coded letters.

e = △ l = ⋈ o = □ t = 8

□h 8ha8 y□u w□u⋈d

b⋈△ss m△ and

△n⧖arg△ my 8△rri8🗨ry

⧖△8 y🗨ur hand

b△ wi8h m△ and

k△△p m△ fr🗨m

harm s🗨 8ha8 I wi⧖⧖

b△ fr△△ fr🗨m pain

God granted his request. We do not know anything else about Jabez. We need to ask God to bless us and to keep us from harm.

OBADIAH

1 Kings 18

Obadiah was a devout believer in the Lord. He worked in the palace of King Ahab of Israel. Jezebel, the queen, hated the prophets of God and tried to have as many as possible killed.

Obadiah took a hundred prophets and hid them in two caves, fifty in each. He brought them food and water every day. His belief in God was put into action.

King Ahab's horses and mules were suffering because of drought. He went to look for water for them and sent Obadiah to do the same. As Obadiah was walking along a certain road, he met with Elijah a famous prophet.

'Go and tell your master, King Ahab, that I am here,' Elijah told Obadiah.

'I am afraid to do that,' replied Obadiah. 'If he knows that I have seen you and you do not turn up at the palace, Ahab will surely kill me.'

'I will certainly go to see King Ahab,' Elijah reassured Obadiah.

So Obadiah took Elijah's message to King Ahab.

What did he tell Elijah?

I	A	N	S	H	L	O	Y	Y
Y	V	T	R	I	E	R	M	O
O	R	H	O	P	H	D	E	U
U	E	A	W	P	T	S	C	T
R	S	V	E	E	D	I	N	H

ASA

1 Kings 15; 2 Chronicles 14

King Asa of Judah was a good man. He obeyed God's laws. He made many improvements in his country and gathered a large army.

One day Asa heard that King Zerah of Ethiopia was on the march with one million soldiers and three hundred chariots. The army prepared for battle but Asa was afraid. His army was much smaller.

Before the battle even started Asa did a wise thing. He prayed to God.

Find your way through the maze to discover part of Asa's prayer. Write it out below.

____

____

Lord	to	help	the	powerless
there	you	like	the	against
is	no	one	mighty	Help
we	for	God	our	us
rely	on	you	Lord	O

The Lord heard Asa's prayer and quickly answered him. The enemy soldiers turned and fled. God gave Asa a great victory.

When we have a problem or difficulty, the best thing that we can do is to pray to God about it.

For over 30 years Asa's land prospered. Near the end of his life he made two big mistakes. First, he relied on a treaty with another king, rather than trusting in God to help him.

What was his other sad mistake? Put the columns in the correct order to find out.

1	2	3	4	5	6	7	8	9	10	11	12	13

7	3	12	9	13	5	11	2	6	10	4	1	8
N	E		H			S	V	I	I	N	E	
S	L		H		E		L	S	E	N	I	
T	D	K	S		N	E	I	O	E		D	
R	L		M				E	F		P	H	O
R	E	T			L	U	H	O	B		T	D
R	L	H	M	E		T	N	F		Y	O	O
C	H		A		S	S	P	I	N	Y		I

NABOTH

1 Kings 21

Naboth owned a beautiful vineyard, close to the palace of wicked King Ahab. Ahab wanted Naboth's vineyard. 'I will pay you for it or I will give you a better one,' said Ahab.

But Naboth did not want to part with his vineyard. It was important to him: it had belonged to his family and Naboth felt it would be wrong to sell his inheritance.

Ahab sulked and raged about Naboth's decision. His wife, Jezebel, was annoyed about it. 'Cheer up,' she said to Ahab, 'I'll get that vineyard for you.' Jezebel told two bad men to make false accusations about Naboth, and he was stoned to death as a punishment.

Immediately Ahab took Naboth's vineyard for himself.

Elijah, the man of God, was sent to Ahab to warn him of the evil consequences of his sin.

Ahab had broken God's law. Which one started the chain of deceit and murder?

Y	O	T	T	H	E	L	U	R	R
O	N	C	Y	I	B	O	O	N	U
U	L	O	N	N	T	N	Y	E	O
S	L	V	A	G	A	G	O	I	B
H	A	E	T	T	H	S	T	G	H

--- ----- --- ----- --------

---- ------- -- ---- ---------

Exodus 20:17

MICAIAH

1 Kings 22; 2 Chronicles 18

King Jehoshaphat of Judah and King Ahab of Israel decided to join together and go to battle against a common enemy.

'We will fight together,' said Jehoshaphat, 'but first let's ask for God's advice.'

Ahab brought 400 prophets to him and asked the question: 'Shall we go to war or not?'

'Go,' they encouraged, 'God will surely give you success.'

Jehoshaphat was not fully convinced. 'Is there not a prophet of the Lord here whom we can ask?' he added.

'There is one man,' said Ahab, 'but I hate him because he never prophesies anything good about me. His name is Micaiah.'

When the other prophets heard that Micaiah was to speak to Ahab, they urged him to give the same message.

What was Micaiah's reply to these other prophets. Read the words in the correct order by joining up the numbers.

1 But
9 lives
12 tell
16 my
6 as
11 can
4 as
3 said
10 I
18 says
13 him
8 Lord
7 the
15 what
5 surely
14 only
17 God
2 Micaiah

Micaiah had to give Ahab the news that when he went to battle he would not return safely. The leader of the false prophets was very angry and slapped Micaiah on the face.

Ahab the king was angry too, and had Micaiah taken away and put in prison with nothing but bread and water.

But Micaiah's words were proved to be true.

GEHAZI

2 Kings 5

Gehazi was the servant of Elisha, the prophet of God in Israel, but he was unlike Elisha in many ways.

Elisha had been used by God to heal the Syrian captain Naaman from leprosy. Naaman was so grateful that he wanted to give Elisha a present. However, he firmly refused any reward.

Gehazi overheard the conversation between his master and Naaman.

'My master was too soft with Naaman,' he thought. 'I will run after him and get something from him.'

When Gehazi caught up with Naaman's party, he made up a story. He said that two men had come to see Elisha and that the prophet needed clothes and money for them.

Naaman gladly gave Gehazi two bags of silver and two sets of clothing. When Gehazi arrived back at the house, he decided to hide the money and clothes.

‘Where have you been?’ asked Elisha on his return.

‘Nowhere,’ lied Gehazi.

Elisha knew very well what his servant had done and his sin was punished severely. Gehazi became a leper and had to leave his master’s service.

What does God think of people who tell lies? Read round the table starting at the arrow.

→ T	H	E	L	O	R	D	D
T	D	E	L	I	G	H	E
U	R	E	T	R	U	T	T
B	A	Prov.	12	22	T	S	E
S	O	L	U	F	H	I	S
P	H	W	N	E	M	N	T
I	L	G	N	I	Y	L	S

JOASH

22 Kings 11; 2 Chronicles 22

Joash, although just a little baby, was the rightful heir to the throne of Judah. His grandmother, Athaliah, was a wicked woman. She plotted to kill the whole royal family, so that she would become queen.

Joash's aunt, Jehosheba, hid him in a bedroom in the temple where she lived with her husband Jehoiada the priest.

Joash grew up in safety in the temple, and was well looked after by his nurse and his aunt. When he was seven years old, Jehoiada the priest made a plan to make Joash king. With the help and protection of the temple guards, Jehoiada brought Joash out of hiding. He put the crown on the little boy's head and proclaimed him king.

What did the crowd of people shout? Unscramble the letters of each word to find out.

NOGL VEIL HET NIGK!

– – – –   – – – –   – – –   – – – – –

Athaliah was furious. What did she shout out? Read the words in the mirror.

Treason!

Treason!

Athaliah was completely defeated. King Joash did what pleased God when his uncle Jehoiada was advising him.

HEZEKIAH

2 Kings 18 and 19

Hezekiah was one of the good kings of Judah. He trusted in God. He kept the commandments that God had given to the people through Moses. God helped him in all that he did.

The king of Assyria was an enemy of the country of Judah then. His army came and conquered a large part of the land. Jerusalem, the capital, was in danger too. The enemy king sent messengers to try and persuade the people of Jerusalem to give up fighting and come over to his side.

Hezekiah's men reported all that they had heard, and showed him the letter from the enemy. Hezekiah was very distressed.

What did Hezekiah do with the letter?
Use the coded word to find the complete message.

L E T T E R

⧗ △ 8 8 △ ◻

H△ ◻△ad I8 8h△n

h△ w△n8 up 8o

8h△ 8△mp⧗△ of 8h△

⧗o◻d. H△ sp◻△ad

I8 ou8 b△fo◻△ 8h△

⧗o◻d and p◻ay△d.

If we have a problem, we too can tell it to the Lord and ask him to help us.

UZZIAH

2 Chronicles 26

Uzziah became king of Judah when he was just 16 years old. He was a good king and pleased God.

Uzziah's kingdom prospered - a big building programme went ahead, the farms were well looked after, and the army was strong.

Follow the arrows to find Uzziah's secret.

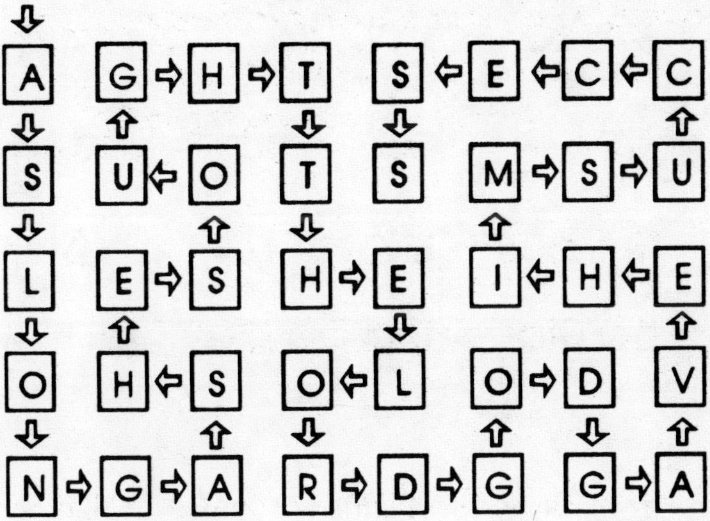

__ ____ __ __ ______

___ ____, ___ ____ ___

________.

After Uzziah became powerful, he became proud. He disobeyed God's laws and became unfaithful to Him. He was angry when his wrongdoing was pointed out.

What a sad end for someone who had begun so well.

MORDECAI

Esther 2 and 6

Mordecai was a Jew who lived far away from his own land in the country we now call Iran. He had brought up his young cousin, Esther, whose mother and father were dead. Esther was very beautiful and became queen of the country.

Mordecai overheard two of the king's guards talking one day. They were plotting to kill the king. He quickly sent a message to queen Esther, who in turn warned the king. Mordecai was given the credit for saving the king's life, and this was reported in the royal record books. But no reward was given to him.

One night much later, the king could not sleep. How would he pass a long night? 'Bring the record book of my reign for me to read,' he ordered.

The king read the account of how Mordecai had saved his life.

'What honour has he received for this?' asked the king.

‘Nothing at all,’ the servants replied.

‘Something should be done for him,’ said the king.

The king asked advice of Haman who was really a very wicked man and an enemy of Mordecai and the Jews. Haman proudly thought that he himself was the man whom the king wanted to honour. So he suggested a wonderful treat. What a shock he had when he discovered that the honour was for Mordecai.

A royal robe was put on Mordecai, and he rode on a royal horse through the city streets. Haman had to walk in front shouting loudly.

What did Haman have to shout? Sort out the columns.

1	2	3	4	5	6	7	8	9	10	11	12

3	9	6	12	1	8	4	11	7	10	2	5
I	A	S	S	T	H	S	I	W	T	H	I
O	T	F			R	N	E	O	H	D	E
A	I	H			K	N	G	E	N	M	T
D	T	I			H	E		G	S		L
T	U	O			O	O		N	R		H

JOB

Job was a very rich man who lived in the land of Uz. He had seven sons and three daughters. He owned many sheep, camels, oxen, donkeys, and had many servants.

Satan watched Job and saw that he was a good man who loved and obeyed God. 'He serves God just because his life is so easy,' said Satan. 'If his pleasant life was taken away, he would probably curse Him instead.' Satan was allowed to put this to the test. 'Do what you want with Job's family and possessions, but do not hurt him,' said God.

How Job's life changed. His oxen and donkeys were attacked by an enemy tribe and carried off. His sheep were destroyed by fire. The camels were taken away by raiding parties. The sons and daughters were feasting in the oldest brother's house. A fierce storm from the desert made the house collapse on top of them and all were killed.

What disasters for Job to face! Did he curse God as Satan had predicted? What did he say?

Read round the spiral, starting from the centre, and work out what Job said.

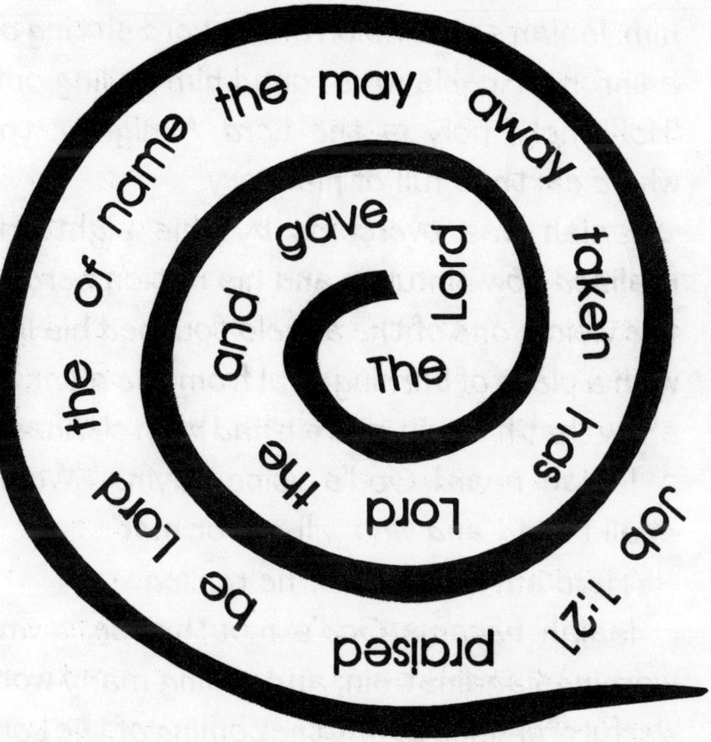
The
Lord
gave
and
the
Lord
has
taken
away
may
the
name
of
the
Lord
be
praised
Job 1:21

He did not sin by blaming God for these disasters.

ISAIAH

Isaiah 6 and 9

Isaiah was a prophet who gave messages from God to the people. He felt unworthy for this important task but God encouraged him. Isaiah saw a vision of the Lord sitting on a throne. Angels were round him calling out, 'Holy, holy, holy is the Lord Almighty; the whole earth is full of his glory.'

Isaiah was overcome by this sight. He realised how sinful he and his nation were. In the vision, one of the angels touched his lips with a piece of burning coal from the altar, to show that his guilt and sin had been cleansed.

Isaiah heard God's voice saying, 'Whom shall I send and who will go for me?'

'Here am I. Send me,' he replied.

Isaiah became God's mouthpiece, giving warnings against sin, and telling many wonderful promises about the coming of the Lord Jesus Christ, and his suffering and death for sinners.

Find one of the many beautiful things that Isaiah told us. Work round the circle noting down every third letter, until all letters are used.

This prophecy came true when Jesus was born.

EBEDMELECH

Jeremiah 38

Jeremiah was a faithful prophet telling the people of Jerusalem God's message. 'Your city will be captured by the Babylonians,' he told them. 'If you stay you will die. But if you go with the Babylonians your life will be spared.' The people did not like this message. They took Jeremiah and lowered him down with ropes into a deep pit. Jeremiah sank down into the mud.

One of the king's servants called Ebedmelech, from north Africa, heard what had happened to Jeremiah. He went to the king to plead on behalf of the prophet. The king listened to Ebedmelech. He told him to take 30 men who would help lift Jeremiah out of the pit.

Ebedmelech found some old rags and worn-out clothes, and threw them down to Jeremiah with the ends of some ropes. 'Put the clothes under your armpits so that the ropes will not hurt you,' he said kindly. Then he and his assistants hauled Jeremiah out of the pit to safety.

Jeremiah was now placed in the courtyard of the guard. When he was there God sent him another message especially for Ebedmelech. The city of Jerusalem was to be taken by the enemy, but God would spare the men who had helped Jeremiah out of the pit.

What did God say to him? Note down the letters corresponding to the hours on the clock face.

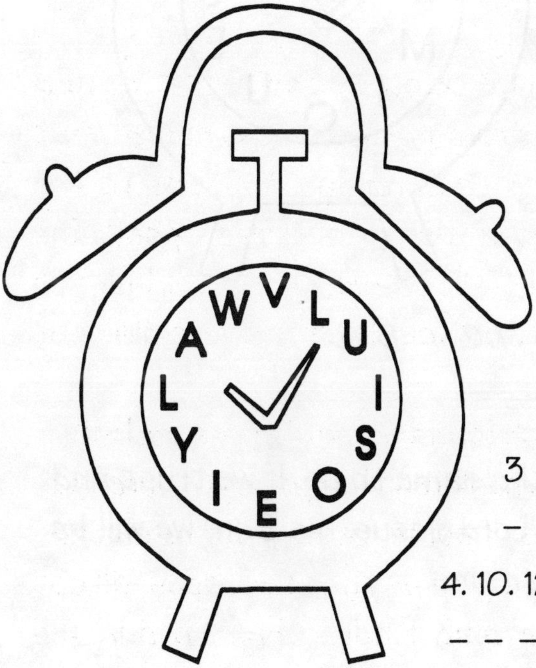

3 11. 7. 9. 1.

_ _ _ _ _

4. 10. 12. 6. 8. 5. 2.

_ _ _ _ _ _ _

Do the same with the second clock to find the next part of God's message.

11. 6. 3.

_ _ _

1. 9. 5. 12. 10   7. 2   8. 4.

_ _ _ _ _   _ _   _ _

God says the same to us. If we trust and believe in the Lord Jesus, his Son, we will be saved from our sins.

EZEKIEL

Ezekiel 1, 4, 5, 34

Ezekiel had been taken as a prisoner from his own land to the country of Babylon. He and other prisoners would meet by the banks of the river Kebar. One day God spoke powerfully to Ezekiel in a vision. He wanted him to speak His word to the Jews who were prisoners in Babylon. Ezekiel did this in a very unusual way, not just by speaking to them, but by acting out situations which symbolised God's message.

Ezekiel lay on his left side for 390 days, and each day counted for 390 years when Israel had sinned. Then he lay on his right side for 40 days - each one symbolising 40 years of sin by the land of Judah.

God told him to cut his hair off and divide it into three piles. One pile had to be burnt, another cut into pieces with a sword, and the third scattered to the wind. Only a few hairs were to be kept. This was to show what would happen to the Jewish people. How people must have wondered at the strange things that Ezekiel did.

Ezekiel warned too, about the leaders who did not look after their people properly.

What was the message that Ezekiel heard from God? Fit the pieces into the jigsaw.

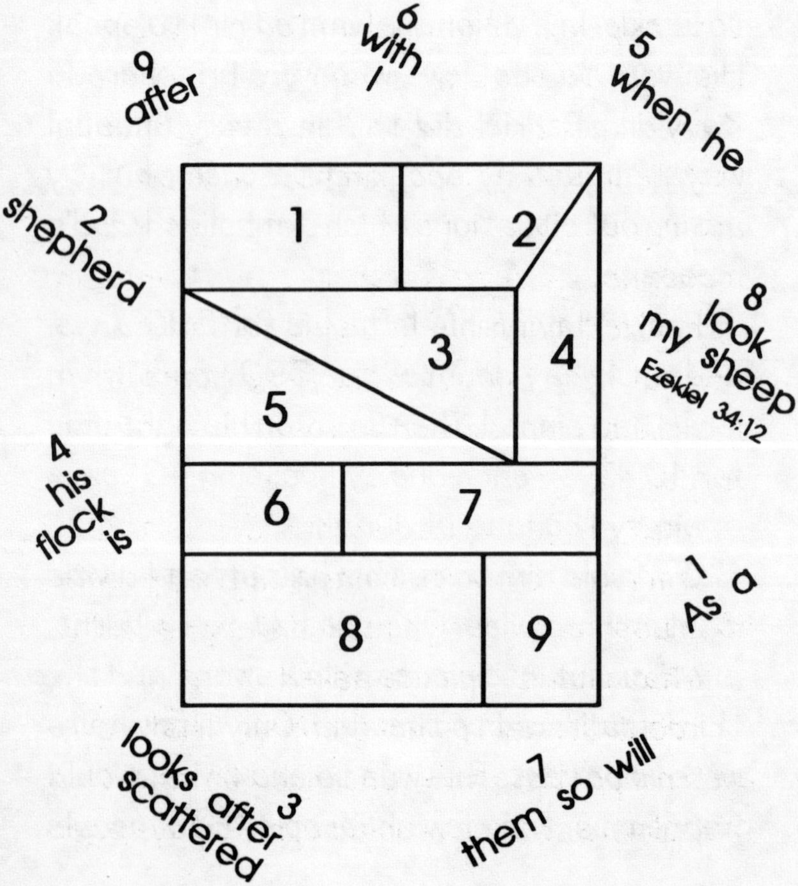

CLEOPAS

Luke 24:13-35

Cleopas and his friend were walking from Jerusalem to Emmaus, a distance of about seven miles. On the road they talked together about the amazing events which had just happened in Jerusalem. Jesus had been crucified three days earlier and they were puzzled and distressed. They had thought that Jesus would be a great leader of their people.

As they talked together, Jesus came up and walked along beside them. He had indeed died but had risen from the dead three days later. Cleopas and his friend did not recognise Jesus.

'What are you talking about?' Jesus asked.

'Don't you know what has been happening in Jerusalem recently?' replied Cleopas sadly.

'What things?' Jesus asked.

'About Jesus,' replied Cleopas. 'That powerful prophet. He was sentenced to death by the rulers and then crucified three days ago.

Some women went to his tomb but could not find his body. They saw angels who said that he was alive. It is all so puzzling.'

'How foolish you are,' said Jesus. 'Don't you believe what the Scriptures say. Jesus Christ had to suffer before he entered glory.'

What did Jesus then do? Work round the grid from the lower left corner, into the centre, to find out.

N	E	D	T	O	T	H
I	H	E	S	C	R	E
A	T	I	M	S	I	M
L	L	H	24	E	P	W
P	L	T	E	L	T	H
X	A	U	K	F	U	A
E	N	O	U	L	R	T
E	I	B	A	S	E	W
H	D	I	A	S	S	A

-- ---------

-- ---- ----

--- ---- --

--- ---

Luke 24:27

Jesus was going to carry on further along the road when they reached Emmaus, but Cleopas and his friend begged him to stay. As they were eating bread together, they realised that the man was Jesus.

NATHANAEL

John 1:43-51

The Lord Jesus chose twelve men to be his special helpers. They were called 'disciples'. Jesus asked Philip to follow him. Philip went to find his friend Nathanael. 'We have found the one that Moses wrote about in the books of the Law, and that the prophets wrote about in their books - he is Jesus from Nazareth,' Philip told him.

'From Nazareth!' exclaimed Nathanael. 'Can anyone good come from that wicked place?'

What did Philip say to Nathanael? Unscramble the letters.

OECM DAN ESE

_ _ _ _ _ _ _ _ _ _

When Jesus saw Nathanael approaching, he greeted him in a way that showed that he already knew him.

'How do you know me?' asked Nathanael in surprise.

'I saw you when you were under the fig tree,' replied Jesus. The shady place under the fig tree was a favourite place for prayer and study.

When Nathanael realised that Jesus knew all about him, he made a bold declaration.

What was it?

___ ___ ___ ___ __ ___: ___
1 2 3 4 5 6 7

___ ___ ____ __ _______ (John1:49)
8 9 10 11 12

NICODEMUS

John 3

Nicodemus was an important man in Jerusalem, a member of the ruling council. He came to see Jesus one night, to find out more about him.

Read round the spiral to find one of the lessons that Jesus taught him.

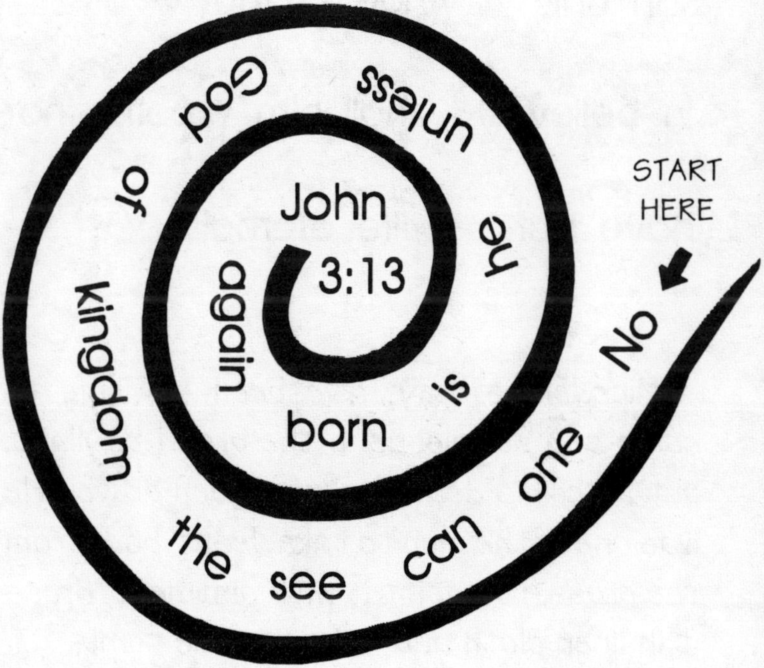
START HERE
No
one
can
see
the
kingdom
of
God
unless
he
is
born
again
John
3:13

Nicodemus found this very hard to understand and Jesus had to explain it to him. Jesus told him plainly about how much God loves people like us.

God for   loved so   world the

he that   his gave   and one

Son only   whoever that

in believes   shall him   perish not

have but   life eternal

Nicodemus may have been unwilling to come and see Jesus in the broad daylight, but after his death he was much braver. He was one of the men to take Jesus' body from the cross, to anoint it with ointment, dress it in linen cloth and bury it in the tomb.

MATTHIAS

Acts 1:15-26

The disciples met together in an upstairs room with Jesus' mother and brothers and some others. They wanted to pray together and discuss the amazing happenings of the previous weeks. Jesus, their master, had died on the cross, but he had risen again from the dead and many of them had seen him. The disciples had also witnessed Jesus being taken from the Mount of Olives up to heaven. What amazing events. What a wonderful Lord and Saviour they had.

One sad fact would have troubled them. Judas Iscariot who had been one of their number, had cruelly betrayed Jesus. Feeling ashamed and guilty about what he had done, he had taken his own life.

After Jesus' ascension, Peter proposed that someone else who had been a witness of Jesus' public ministry until his ascension, should be chosen to replace Judas.

Two men were proposed: Barnabas and

Matthias. The disciples prayed that God would guide them to the right man.

What was their prayer? Unscramble each word.

OLDR UOY NWOK EOYREVESN TEHRA.

WHOS SU CHHIW FO SEHTE

WOT OUY VEAH HECOSN

They cast lots and Matthias was chosen. He joined the other eleven disciples.

BARNABAS

Acts 4, 9, 11, 13, 15

Barnabas came from the island of Cyprus. He sold a field which he owned and brought the money to the apostles to be used for the Christians who were in need.

He was well educated and highly respected. Barnabas introduced Paul to the church in Jerusalem after his conversion. They were suspicious of him but Barnabas reassured them of his changed life.

Barnabas was a very encouraging person. *What did he encourage the Christians at Antioch to do? Take every fourth letter, starting with T.*

Barnabas was a good man, full of the Holy Spirit and faith. God used him and his preaching.

What was the result? Use the code to find out.

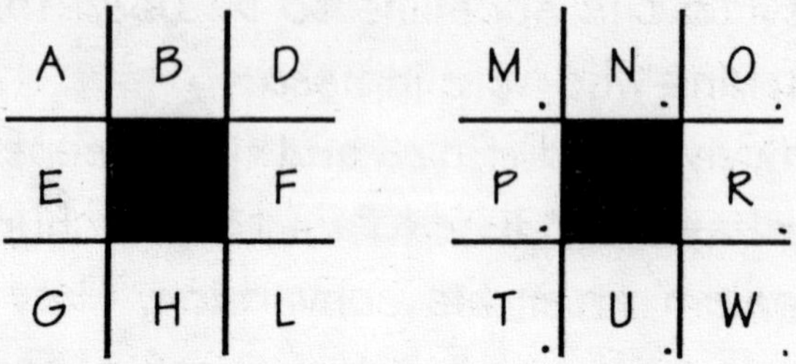

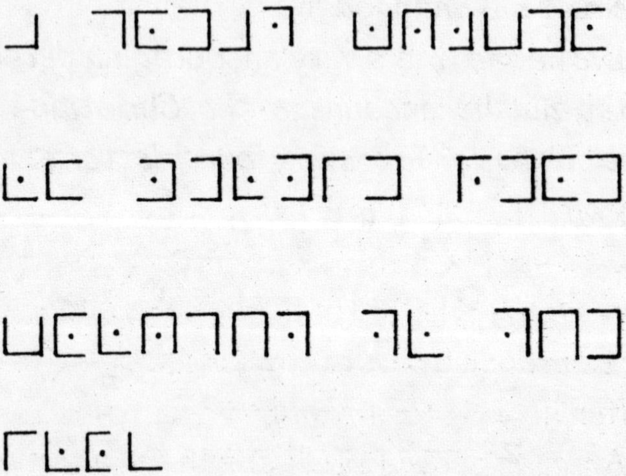

Barnabas became a travelling missionary, and went on long preaching tours with Paul.

ANANIAS

Acts 9

Ananias lived in Damascus. He was a follower of the Lord Jesus. One day God spoke to him in a vision. God told him 'Go to Judas' house on Straight Street and ask to see a man called Saul from Tarsus. He is praying. He has seen in a vision that you will come to him. You must place your hands on him and restore his sight.'

Ananias was alarmed when he heard this. 'I have heard of Saul,' he replied to the Lord. 'He has done a lot of harm to those who love you. I believe he has come to Damascus to arrest those of us who love you.'

God spoke firmly to Ananias. 'Go!' he said. Then he added, 'This man has been chosen by me to preach my word to many people. He will suffer greatly for my sake.'

Ananias obeyed God's command and made his way to the house where he met Saul whose life had been dramatically changed. Ananias explained to Saul why he had come.

Discover what Annanias said to Saul by working your way through the grid. Start at The.

The	to	you	on	here	has	sent
Lord	appeared	road	the	coming	so	me
Jesus	who	as	you	were	that	you
9	Chapter	Holy	the	be	and	may
verse 17	Acts	spirit	with	filled	again	see

___ ____ _____ ___

________ __ ___ __ ___

____ __ ___ ____ ______

____, ___ ____ __ __ ____

___ ___ ___ _____ ___ __

______ ____ ___ ____

______ (Acts 9:17)

Saul, who had been blind for three days, was immediately able to see again.

DORCAS

Acts 9:36-43

Dorcas was a very popular person in Joppa. She was a clever lady and spent a lot of her time sewing clothes for needy people. Those who were orphans or widows were very grateful to Dorcas for her lovely gifts of clothes.

Dorcas became sick and died. Her body was washed and laid in an upstairs room. Her friends sent immediately for the apostle Peter. He had been used to healing people who were sick. Perhaps he could do something for Dorcas.

When Peter arrived he was taken upstairs to the room where Dorcas was lying. Many of the mothers whom she had helped, came to him weeping. They showed Peter the clothes that she had made.

Peter sent them all out of the room. He knelt down and prayed to God. He said to Dorcas, 'Get up!' She opened her eyes, saw Peter and sat up. What a wonderful miracle. What joy when her friends and neighbours met with her again. The good news spead all over the town.

What was the result? Solve the code.

1	2	3	4	5	6	7	8	9	10	11	12	13
A	B	C	D	E	F	G	H	I	J	K	L	M

14	15	16	17	18	19	20	21	22	23	24	25	26
N	O	P	Q	R	S	T	U	V	W	X	Y	Z

13.1.14.25. 16.5.15.16.12.5.

_ _ _ _ _ _ _ _ _ _

2.5.12.9.5.22.5.4. 9.14. 20.8.5.

_ _ _ _ _ _ _ _ _ _ _ _ _

12.15.18.4.

_ _ _ _

RHODA

Acts 12:12-17

Peter the preacher was put in prison by wicked King Herod. His Christian friends prayed earnestly to God for him.

The night before he was due to stand trial, Peter was miraculously delivered from the prison by an angel - out of the chains, past the guards, through the doors and gates - right out into the street.

He made his way to the house belonging to John Mark's mother, Mary. Many people had gathered there to pray for Peter. Peter knocked at the door. A servant girl called Rhoda went to answer. She was so excited when she recognised Peter's voice that she forgot to open the door. Instead she ran back into the house to tell the good news to the gathering.

'You're mad!' someone said. 'It must be his angel,' said someone else. But Peter kept on knocking and eventually somebody had the sense to open the door. Rhoda had been right. There was Peter.

What did Peter do? Find out by reading round the grid, strarting at P.

T	I	O	N	E	D	W	I	T	H	H
O	T	A	N	D	D	E	S	C	R	I
M	E	A	D	B	R	O	U	G	I	S
R	I	H	F	P	R	I	S	H	B	H
E	U	D	O			N	O	T	E	A
T	Q	R	T	U	O	M	I	H	D	N
E	E	O	L	E	H	T	W	O	H	D
P	B	O	T	M	E	H	T	R	O	F

_____ ________ ____ ___

____ ___ ____ __ __

_____ ___ _________ ___

___ ____ ___ _______

___ ___ __ ______ (Acts 12:17)

What a wonderful answer to prayer.

LYDIA

Acts 16:11-15

Lydia was a business woman who lived and worked in Philippi. She was a seller of expensive purple cloth.

Lydia regularly met with other women at a quiet place by the riverside, and there they prayed to God. One day Paul and his friends went to meet this prayer group. Paul sat down with them and spoke earnestly about the gospel message. Lydia listened to the message and trusted in the Lord Jesus as her Saviour.

Why did she respond? Work round the spiral from the centre.

--- ----

------ ---

(Acts 16:14)

T H E L O R D O P E N E D H E R H E A R T

Lydia and her family were baptised, and she invited Paul and his fellow-travellers to her home to stay. She showed love and friendship to other Christians.

Paul and his colleague, Silas, were soon put in prison for preaching the gospel but were miraculously saved by God. When they came out of prison, they stayed again at Lydia's house. There they met with the church people and encouraged them. Lydia was practising what Jesus had asked his followers to do,

Work round the spiral from the outside into the centre.

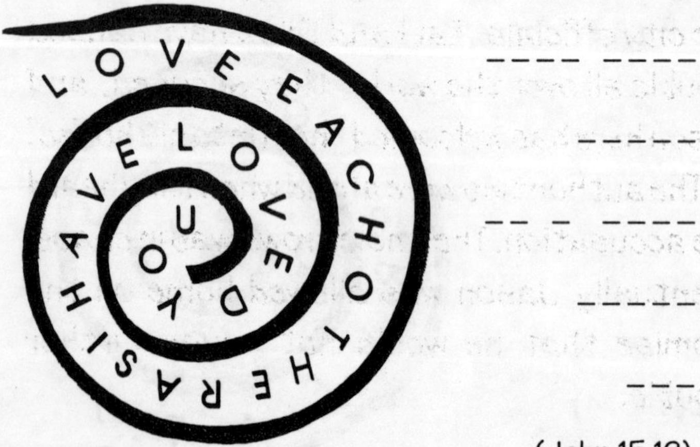
LOVEEACHOTHERASIHAVELOVEDYOU

(John 15:12)

JASON

Acts 17:5-9

Paul and Silas came to Thessalonica on their missionary journey. They preached to the people, explaining that Jesus had died and risen from the dead, and proving that he was the Christ sent from God. Some people believed in the Lord Jesus Christ as a result, but many of the Jews were jealous and angry.

Some Jews gathered a rowdy mob of bad men and started a riot in the town. They rushed to Jason's house where they expected to find Paul and Silas, but they were not there. Instead, they dragged Jason to the city officials. 'Paul and Silas have caused trouble all over the world,' they accused, 'and Jason here has welcomed them into his house.'

The authorities were afraid when they heard the accusation. The whole crowd was in chaos. Eventually, Jason was allowed home on the promise that he would not cause further trouble.

Which part of Paul's message (which Jason agreed with) upset the officials so much?

Change the symbols to the letters shown.

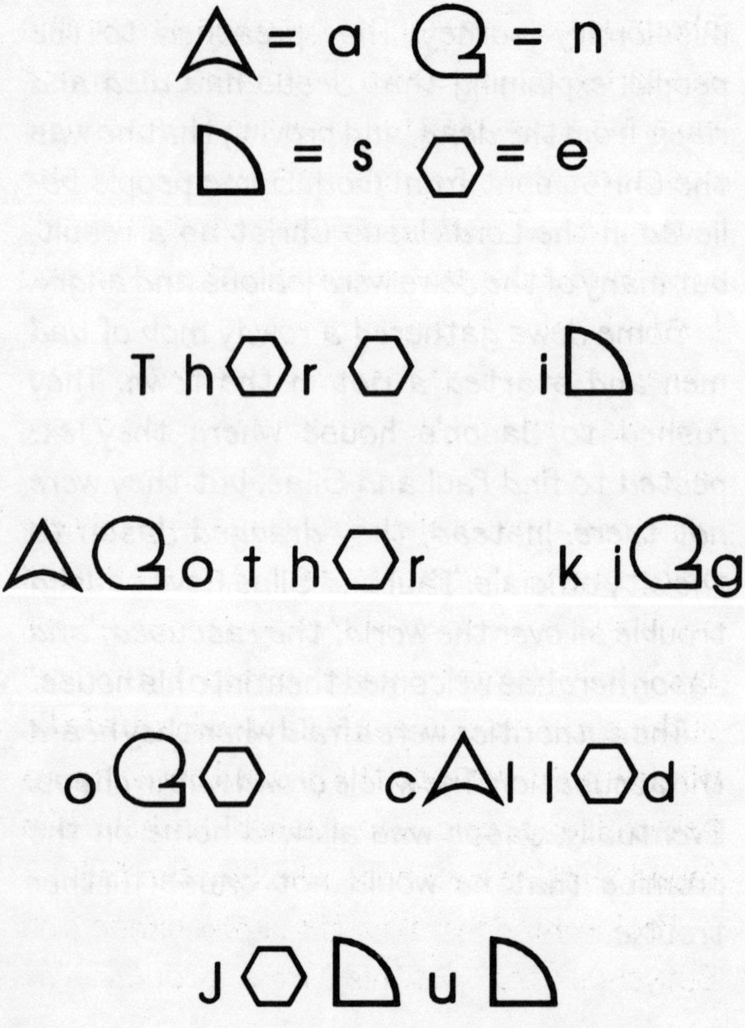

EUTYCHUS

Acts 20:7-12

Paul the missionary preached the good news about Jesus Christ in many towns all over the eastern Mediterranean countries. On one of his trips, he stayed for a week in Troas on the coast of what we now call Turkey. On the Lord's Day (Sunday) a congregation gathered in an upstairs room and they had the Lord's Supper together.

Paul was going to leave on his travels the next day, and so he spoke until it was very late.

A young man called Eutychus was sitting up on an open window ledge. As Paul talked on, Eutychus became more and more sleepy. Eventually he fell sound asleep. He moved suddenly in his sleep and toppled out of the window right down to the ground three floors below. The people who rushed to help him found that he had been killed by the fall.

Paul went down too. He threw himself on Eutychus and put his arms around him.

'Don't be afraid,' he said to the crowd, 'he's alive.'

God had given Paul the amazing power to raise Eutychus from the dead.

The company went back upstairs where they talked until the morning. What a wonderful miracle of God they would have spoken about.

What did Eutychus and the people do after Paul left? Solve the coded message.

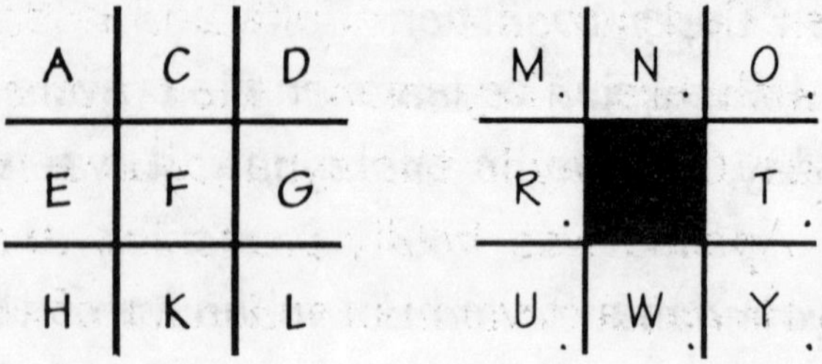

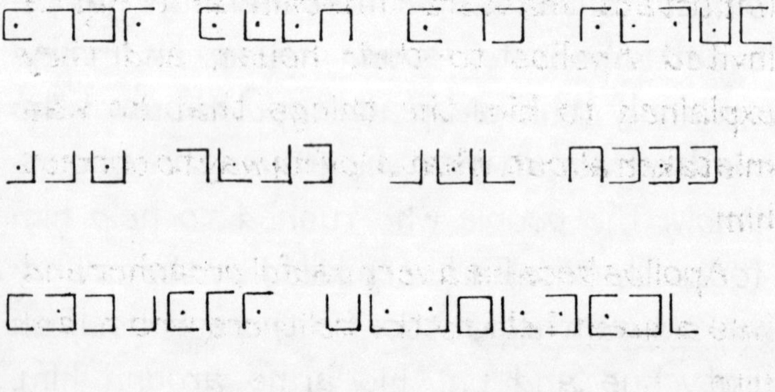

AQUILA AND PRISCILLA

Acts 18

Aquila and his wife Priscilla were tent-makers by trade. While they were living in Corinth they met Paul who was on one of his missionary journeys. Paul stayed with them and worked in the tent-making business. He preached in the synagogue too, trying to persuade people to believe in the Lord Jesus.

When Paul moved on, Aquila and Priscilla went with him. They made their home in Ephesus. One day in the synagogue a man called Apollos was boldly preaching about Jesus. He was a clever man and much of what he said was true but he was wrong on some important matters. Priscilla and Aquila invited Apollos to their house, and they explained to him the things that he was mistaken about. What a loving way to correct him.

Apollos became a very useful preacher and was a great help to the believers who heard him.

What did he do? Put columns in the correct places.

1	2	3	4	5	6	7	8	9	10	11	12	13

4	8	5	1	12	7	10	3	13	2	6	9	11
R	D	O	H	M	E	R	P		E	V	F	O
S	P	C	T	E	I	U	E	S	H	R	T	R
T	U	J	T	S	S	W	A		H	E	S	A
H	R	E			H	S	T			C	I	T

__ ______ ____ ___ __________

____ ______ ___ ___ ______

(Acts 18:28)

PAUL'S NEPHEW

Acts 23:12-22

Paul the missionary preached about the Lord Jesus in many places. Some people began to love the Lord Jesus because of Paul's preaching, but others disagreed with what he said and hated Paul too.

In Jerusalem, Paul spoke boldly to crowds of people and to the Jewish leaders. Forty Jewish men made a plan to get rid of Paul. 'We will not eat or drink,' they vowed, 'until we have killed him.'

Paul's nephew, his sister's son, learned about the plot. He rushed to the barracks where Paul was held prisoner, and told him what he had heard.

Paul called one of the soldiers, 'Take my nephew to the commander; he has something to tell him.'

The young man passed on his information to the commander, who immediately acted on it. Paul was taken at night out of the prison and transferred to another town.

The wicked plot to kill Paul was foiled by the quick action of the young man, Paul's nephew.

Where was Paul sent? Before which official did he stand trial? Starting at C, follow the arrows to find out.

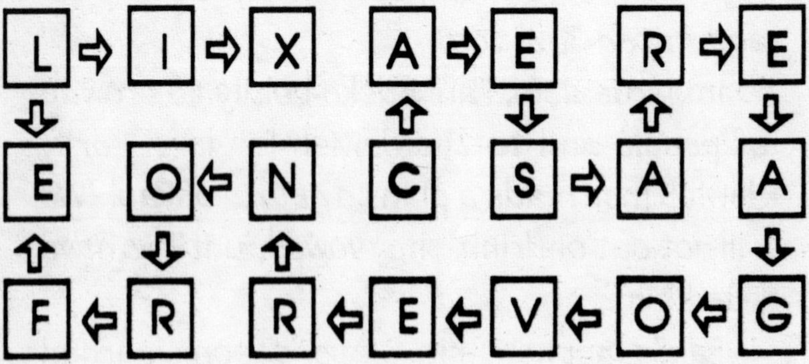

_ _ _ _ _ _ _ _

_ _ _ _ _ _ _ _   _ _ _ _ _

PHOEBE

Romans 16:1-2

Phoebe was a lady who worked for the church in a town called Cenchrea, six miles east of Corinth.

She was given the responsible task of carrying Paul's letter to the Christians at Rome. Paul asked the Roman believers to welcome her warmly in a way worthy of a saint.

He asked them also to give her any help that she might need. Why?

Follow the arrows:

↓	S	E	E	T	H	A	N	E
	H	B	N	A	E	M	Y	L
	E	S	A	E	L	O	P	P
	H	A	G	R	P	T	E	O

LOIS AND EUNICE

2 Timothy 1:5

Paul wrote two letters to his friend and colleague, Timothy. Timothy was a younger man but Paul was greatly impressed by his faith in, and zeal for God.

Paul knew that Timothy would have been taught well by his grandmother Lois and his mother Eunice. They both had a strong faith in the Lord Jesus, and passed on the good news of the Bible to Timothy.

Join up the trail to find out what Paul said about Timothy.

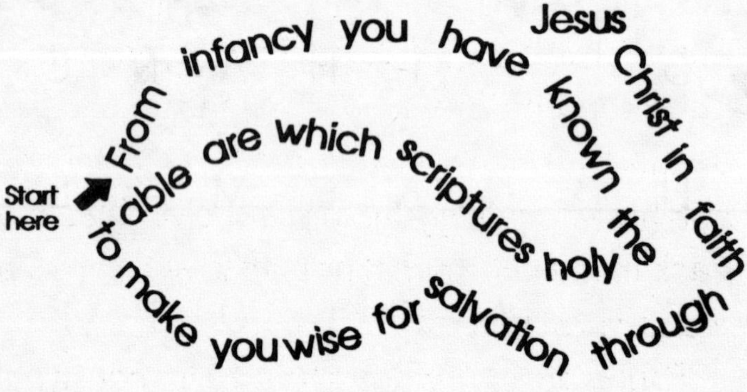
Start here
From
infancy
you
have
known
the
holy
scriptures
which
are
able
to
make
you
wise
for
salvation
through
faith
in
Christ
Jesus

It is good for you to learn God's word when you are young too - like Timothy did.

ONESIMUS

Philemon

Onesimus was a slave. He would have to do exactly as he was told - working hard from morning till night.

One day, Onesimus rebelled. He stole from Philemon, his master, and ran away, hoping for a better life away from slavery.

His travelling brought him in touch with Paul the preacher, and from that day his life was completely changed. He heard the good news of the Lord Jesus and his death on the cross for sinners. Onesimus was sorry for his sin and turned to God by faith in Jesus Christ. He decided to return to his master Philemon who was also a believer in the Lord Jesus. Paul wrote a tactful letter to Philemon and his wife asking them to receive Onesimus back into their home, not as a slave, but as a dear brother.

Paul was confident that Philemon would welcome Onesimus back.

Why was Paul so confident about this? What did Philemon have that made all the difference?

	1	2	3	4	5	6	7	8	9	10	11	12
a	F			T	H			N		T	H	
b		L		R	D		J		S		S	

Put the vowels in the correct places in the grid.

A: 2a,
E: 12a, 8b,
I: 3a, 7a,
O: 3b,
U: 10b

Some of the characters you have been learning about are hidden in the grid. Find them and score them out.

H	T	L	E	O	R	H	T	E	J	H	J
T	H	Y	B	E	N	G	O	O	A	D	O
E	E	D	E	A	S	A	A	I	B	S	B
H	Z	I	D	Q	R	S	D	L	E	A	A
S	E	A	M	U	H	N	E	T	Z	C	B
O	K	U	E	I	S	M	A	A	K	R	I
B	I	E	L	L	O	I	S	B	M	O	G
I	A	A	E	A	N	A	H	C	A	D	A
H	H	N	C	C	L	E	O	P	A	S	I
P	I	N	H	T	O	B	A	N	O	U	L
E	R	J	O	C	H	A	B	E	D	I	M
M	A	E	U	T	Y	C	H	U	S	G	E

MEPHIBOSHETH
ABIGAIL
EUTYCHUS
LOIS
CLEOPAS
LYDIA

JOB
AQUILA
JABEZ
JETHRO
JOASH
DORCAS

EBEDMELECH
ACHAN
NABOTH
JOCAHBED
HEZEKIAH
BARNABAS

Once you have found the names, the remaining letters spell out the part of the Bible which first mentions man.

____ ___ ____ ___ __ ____

___ __ ___ ______. (Genesis 1:26)

ANSWERS

ANSWERS

PAGE

7 Introduction

All Scripture is God-breathed and is useful for teaching, rebuking, correcting and training in righteousness.
2 Timothy 3:16.

8 Amram and Jochabed

Moses

10 Jethro

Praise be to the Lord now I know that the Lord is greater than all other gods.
Exodus 18:10-11.

12 Bezalel and Oholiab

Crafts. Woodwork. Weaving. Embroidery. Designing. Jewel setting. Metalwork. Teaching.

14 Rahab

The Lord your God is God in heaven above and on earth below. Joshua 2:11.

16 Achan

Do not be afraid; do not be discouraged.
Joshua 8:1.

18 Mephibosheth

Do not be afraid for I will surely show you kindness. 2 Samuel 9:7.
He always ate at the king's table. 2 Samuel 9:13.

21 Nathan

Wash away all my iniquity and cleanse me from my sin. Psalm 51:2.

23 Abigail

Your life will be bound securely in the bundle of the living by the Lord your God. 1 Samuel 25:29.

26 Jabez

Oh that you would bless me and enlarge my territory! Let your hand be with me

28 Obadiah

I your servant have worshipped the Lord since my youth. 1 Kings 18:12.

30 Asa

Lord there is no one like you to help the powerless against the mighty. Help us, O Lord our God for we rely on you. 2 Chronicles 14:11.

PAGE

30 Even in his illness he did not seek help from the Lord but only from the physi cians. 2 Chronicles 16:12.

33 NABOTH

You shall not covet anything that be longs to your neighbour. Exodus 20:17.

35 MICAIAH

But Micaiah said, As surely as the Lord lives, I can tell him only what my God says. 2 Chronicles 18:13.

37 GEHAZI

The Lord detests lying lips but he delights in men who are truthful. Proverbs 12:22.

39 JOASH

Long live the king! 2 Kings 11:12.
Treason. Treason. 2 Kings 11:14.

41 HEZEKIAH

He read it then he went up to the temple of the Lord and spread it out before the Lord. And prayed to the Lord. 2 Kings 19:14, 15.

43 *Uzziah*

As long as he sought the Lord, God gave him success. 2 Chronicles 26:5.

45 *Mordecai*

This is what is done for the man the king delights to honour. Esther 6:11.

48 *Job*

The Lord gave and the Lord has taken away may the name of the Lord be praised. Job 1:21.

50 *Isaiah*

For to us a child is born, to us a son is given. Isaiah 9:6.

52 *Ebedmelech*

I will save you. You trust in me.
Genesis 39:18

55 *Ezekiel*

As a shepherd looks after his scattered flock when he is with them, so will I look after my sheep. Ezekiel 34:12.

57 *Cleopas*

He explained to them what was said in all the scriptures about himself.
Luke 24.27.

PAGE

59 NATHANAEL

Come and see. John 1:39.
You are the Son of God: you are the king of Israel. John 1:49.

61 NICODEMUS

No one can see the kingdom of God unless he is born again. John 3:3.
For God so loved the world that he gave his one and only Son that whoever be lieves in him shall not perish but have eternal life. John 3:16.

63 MATTHIAS

Lord you know everyone's heart. Show us which of these two you have chosen. Acts 1:24.

65 BARNABAS

To remain true to the Lord with all their hearts. Acts 11:23.
A great number of people were brought to the Lord. Acts 11:21.

67 ANANIAS

The Lord Jesus who appeared to you on the road as you were coming here, has sent me so that you may see again and be filled with the Holy Spirit. Acts 9:17.

69 Dorcas

Many people believed in the Lord.
Acts 9:42.

71 Rhoda

Peter motioned with his hand for them to be quiet and described how the Lord had brought him out of prison.
Acts 12:17.

73 Lydia

The Lord opened her heart. Acts 16:14.
Love each other as I have loved you.
John 15:12.

75 Jason

There is another king, one called Jesus.
Acts 17:7.

77 Eutychus

They took the young man home and were greatly comforted. Acts 20:12

79 Aquila and Priscilla

He proved from the scriptures that Jesus was the Christ. Acts 18:28.

81 Paul's nephew

Caesarea.
Governor Felix.

PAGE

83 *Phoebe*

She has been a great help to many people. Romans 16:2

84 *Lois and Eunice*

From infancy you have known the holy scriptures which are able to make you wise for salvation through faith in Christ Jesus. 2 Timothy 3:15

85 *Onesimus*

Faith in the Lord Jesus. Philemon 5

88 Then God said, 'Let us make man in our image.' Genesis 1:26.